Assessing Quality in
EARLY CHILDHOOD EDUCATION AND CARE

Sustained Shared Thinking and Emotional Well-being (SSTEW) Scale for 2–5-year-olds provision

Iram Siraj, Denise Kingston & Edward Melhuish

Foreword by Kathy Sylva

A Trentham Book

IOEPress

Trentham Books

First published in 2015 by IOE Press, UCL Institute of Education, University College London, 20 Bedford Way, London WC1H 0AL

ioepress.co.uk

© Iram Siraj, Denise Kingston and Edward Melhuish

British Library Cataloguing in Publication Data:
A catalogue record for this publication is available from the British Library

ISBNs
978-1-85856-658-0 (paperback)
978-1-85856-665-8 (PDF eBook)

Cover and text designed and set by emc design ltd
Printed by CPI Group (UK) Ltd, Croydon, CR0 4YY

Cover image ©iStock.com/CEFutcher

Authors

Iram Siraj is a Professor at the UCL Institute of Education and a visiting Professor at the University of Wollongong. She co-led on the Effective Pre-school, Primary and Secondary Education (EPPSE) longitudinal study, and the highly influential Researching Effective Pedagogy in the Early Years (REPEY) study, which first developed the concept of Sustained Shared Thinking (SST). She is a co-author of the ECERS-E and has published widely on quality, pedagogy, and curriculum.

Denise Kingston is a Senior Lecturer at the University of Brighton and a Senior Researcher at the UCL Institute of Education. She is a qualified educational psychologist and teacher and has worked as a schools psychologist and advisory teacher supporting inclusion and as a Portage supervisor and visitor. She has extensive experience of training on environment rating scales.

Edward Melhuish is a Professor at the University of Oxford and Birkbeck, University of London, and a visiting Professor at the University of Wollongong. He co-led the National Evaluation of Sure Start, the Effective Pre-school, Primary and Secondary Education (EPPSE) project and is currently undertaking the Study of Early Education and Development (SEED) project. His research has influenced policy on childcare, early education, child poverty, and parental support in the UK and other countries.

Acknowledgements

The SSTEW Scale has benefitted considerably from feedback by expert practitioners and academics from across the globe and through trial in early childhood settings by a huge number of people. We cannot mention everyone by name, but we would like to thank all of those who gave us their time and input. This includes the Early Years Teaching Team and MA Education (Early Childhood) students (Stage 1: 2013/2014) at the School of Education, University of Brighton. Also, the teachers in the early years leaders subject network (2013–14) for the Brighton Partnership in Leadership and Learning, and in particular Helen Filson from St Luke's Primary School.

We received excellent support from the researchers on the Study of Early Education and Development (SEED) project in England and from many of the staff at the University of Wollongong in Australia, especially Dr Steven Howard and A/Professor Pauline Lysaght. We thank staff from the Australian NSW Department of Education and Communities (DEC), especially Philippa Becker and her team, and colleagues from the University of Macquarie, including Sandra Cheeseman. From London we had great feedback from many colleagues, including Carol Archer, an advisory teacher in Camden.

We are grateful to Professor Collette Tayler from the Melbourne Graduate School of Education and Professor Kathy Sylva from Oxford University for their encouragement, comments, and support.

Contents

Read before you start

Foreword

The **Sustained Shared Thinking and Emotional Well-being (SSTEW) Scale** is an exciting new observational tool for assessing practice in centre-based early education and care. Based on new findings from the developmental sciences, this innovative scale describes educational practices that support the development of task focus, problem-solving, and imagination. Earlier scales have assessed the quality of space and resources, activities, and curricular provision. What this new scale adds to the current 'tool-kit' of quality assessment is a welcome focus on well-being, self-regulation, and the kind of focused thinking in children that is supported through sensitive interactions with others. The 14 items in this scale consist of clearly defined 'indicators', showing an incline of quality in practice.

The first two sub-scales assess the quality of provision for children's autonomy and socio-emotional development. Carefully graded indicators within each item allow a clear analytic lens to be focused on daily practices that support the development of trust in young children and the capacity to deal positively with distress or conflict. However, the first two sub-scales do not assume that practitioners wait for distress or conflict to occur before acting; they acknowledge that practitioners in high-quality centres create environments that keep children positively engaged in interesting activities and interactions. The sub-scales recognize the ways in which staff encourage collaborative play and develop consistent strategies for helping children think through and resolve conflicts. Thus, clearly articulated 'indicators' of good practice in each item guide assessors as they make judgements about quality to be used in research, professional development, or audit.

The following three sub-scales focus on practices that support the development of 'executive' skills in children such as task focus, emotional regulation, and setting and achieving goals. Sustained shared thinking refers to the capacity to work with others in coherent and sustained ways towards a goal or resolution. The three sub-scales on sustained shared thinking assess practice that enables children to interact in collaboration with others as they solve problems or express themselves. The scale's indicators describe ways in which staff engage in conversations or play that allow the partners to build on each other's actions, ideas, and intentions. All of the items on sustained shared thinking describe the things adults do to support children in working with others to explore and understand the world.

The five sub-scales that comprise the scale seem at first to be wholly separate, with personal and emotional items at the beginning and intellectual items towards the end. However, careful study of the scale reveals a coherent underlying theory. Practices that support emotional development as well as task focus in problem-solving all rest on *communication* between adult and child. Narrative is important here but so too is guided thinking based on open questions and the sharing of views. The complex communication described so richly in the scale is multilayered in its focus on the external world, the world of things and events, but also on the internal world of feelings and wishes. The discrete items in this scale are all based on communication, and it is this that provides coherence and the rationale for the inclines of quality in practice.

Kathy Sylva
Professor of Educational Psychology, University of Oxford

Introduction to the Sustained Shared Thinking and Emotional Well-being (SSTEW) Scale

This is an environment rating scale that can be used for research, self-evaluation and improvement, audit and regulation. It has a similar scoring framework to the family of Environmental Rating Scales (ERSs) first developed in the USA; for example, the Early Childhood Environment Rating Scale – Revised (ECERS-R) (Harms et al., 2005) and the Infant/Toddler Environment Rating Scale – Revised (ITERS-R) (Harms et al., 2003). It is also closely linked with the Early Childhood Environment Rating Scale – Extension (ECERS-E) (Sylva et al., 2010). Anyone who has been trained on earlier environment rating scales should find SSTEW relatively easy to use as it has a similar format; the content, however, will require bespoke training from authorized trainers.

The environment rating scales that have been developed to support practice within early years provision for children aged from birth to 5 years have traditionally been based on the notion of developmentally appropriate practice (DAP) prevalent at the time. Over the years they have been adapted and extended as research has improved our knowledge of what constitutes effective practice. For instance, ECERS-E was designed as an extension to ECERS-R and included new ideas about the importance of further supporting academic outcomes. It covered areas of the curriculum – literacy, numeracy, and science and the environment – together with a sub-scale on diversity to ensure that early childhood staff planned for the needs of individuals and groups of children. ECERS-R and ECERS-E together provide observed measures of the physical, social, and emotional environment, as well as assessing pedagogical and curricular practices designed to support emergent cognitive functioning (Burchinal et al., 2008; Howes et al., 2008; Mashburn et al., 2008).

Over the years, many national and international studies have shown that the environment rating scales are reliable and valid and, most importantly, related to children's socio-emotional and cognitive development (Burchinal et al., 2002; Phillipsen et al., 1997; Sylva et al., 2004). However, more recent research on effective settings, e.g. the Effective Provision of Pre-school Education (EPPE) study, has indicated that it is important to consider other aspects of development and practice when supporting children's learning and development and promoting children's outcomes (Siraj-Blatchford et al., 2002; Siraj-Blatchford, 2009). The latter studies promoted the concept of 'sustained shared thinking' (SST), the active engagement of practitioners in children's learning and extending thinking, which has been widely used in many curricula across the world. It has influenced the English Early Years Foundation Stage (EYFS) (Early Education, 2012) and key work in other countries, for instance, the Australian Early Years Learning Framework (EYLF) (DEEWR and CAG, 2009). Yet the practices associated with SST are still relatively poor, despite knowing that it is a pedagogical strategy strongly associated with child outcomes (Siraj-Blatchford et al., 2002; Sylva et al., 2004). This scale is designed to consider practice that supports children aged between 2 and 5 years of age in developing skills in sustained shared thinking and emotional well-being as well as in developing strong relationships, effective communication, and aspects of self-regulation.

The SSTEW Scale has been trialled by many practitioners, and by academics involved in early childhood research, and is currently being used in over 1,000 settings in the Study of Early Education and Development (SEED) project in England. Therefore, further information on reliability and predictive validity will be published in the second edition of the Scale.

Rationale for the development of the SSTEW Scale

The term 'sustained shared thinking' was first coined by Siraj-Blatchford et al. (2002) during the qualitative analysis of data (through narratives of observed and recorded interactions within 12 good and excellent pre-school 'outlier' settings) collected by the Researching Effective Pedagogy in the Early Years (REPEY) project. This was a sister project to the Effective Provision of Pre-school Education (EPPE) longitudinal study (Sylva et al., 2004). Being able to engage in sustained shared thinking with a child was recognized as a key skill of the staff in pre-school settings who were effective in supporting children's socio-emotional and cognitive outcomes. The definition of sustained shared thinking within this project was:

An episode in which two or more individuals 'work together' in an intellectual way to solve a problem, clarify a concept, evaluate activities, extend a narrative, etc. Both parties must contribute to the thinking and it must develop and extend.

Since that time, the definition of sustained shared thinking (SST) has been developed further and has naturally been extended from its original position of purely relating to the narrative research data in REPEY. So, for example, SST has been applied to episodes of non-verbal interactions where two or more individuals work together, particularly in relation to younger children and babies or children with English as an additional language (EAL). The key concept of a sustained 'contribution to thinking' was originally aligned to pre-existing ideas regarding the support children need to learn and develop, such as those found in the Vygotskian concept of the zone of proximal development (ZPD) (see Siraj-Blatchford et al., 2002; Siraj-Blatchford, 2009). This, together with the examples of SST noted in REPEY, led some people to consider extended periods of exchanges or long conversations as a requirement and essential to SST. However, when the emphasis is placed on 'a contribution to thinking',

it becomes obvious that this can happen when exchanges are few and can take place between children as well as between children and adults. In terms of the adult role, what becomes essential is the sensitive, child-centred intervention of the adult when supporting the child's learning and development. This may include 'standing back' and allowing the child to explore, familiarize, solve problems, and think by themselves or in pairs as well as intervening and supporting the child through Vygotsky's zone of proximal development (ZPD).

Research that considers effective settings (that is, settings that support and enhance children's developmental outcomes) recognizes the skills of practitioners, and therefore how they interact with children and support their learning and development, as the most important element of high quality. Engaging in SST, which includes the successful support of a child's thinking and learning, undoubtedly requires a highly skilled and knowledgeable practitioner. A practitioner who is skilled in assessing, monitoring and supporting children's socio-emotional, linguistic, and cognitive development and who also ensures that the child feels safe, comfortable, interested and stimulated, as these are necessary conditions for the child to be ready to learn (Melhuish, 2004) and to be in a position to think deeply. Again, research into effective settings supports the notion that engaging with both care and education equally supports quality (Sylva et al., 2004); where there is only emphasis on care and emotional well-being, children do not make much progress cognitively. It is for these reasons that sustained shared thinking together with social and emotional well-being are included in the scale. To engage in SST with children successfully, the practitioner requires a clear understanding of their current development, cultural heritage and achievements, and their feelings, behaviours and responses to learning. The practitioner needs to be able to recognize when the child is thinking, and sensitively extend periods of concentration and support perseverance. This means the context must be sensitive to the gender, social class, racial and cultural background of each child. Adult–child and child–child relationships and parental partnerships are key to this.

The developmental domains pertinent to SSTEW are:

1   **Social and emotional development**. Two sub-scales relate to this domain: *1. Building trust, confidence, and independence* and *2. Social and emotional well-being*.

2   **Cognitive development**. This is subdivided into language and communication development with the sub-scale: *3. Supporting and extending language and communication* and more general cognitive development with the two sub-scales, *4. Supporting learning and critical thinking*, and *5. Assessing learning and language*.

While there are important differences in development between children aged 2–5 years, we believe that there are common practices that will support and nurture children within this age range when suitably adapted to the individuals involved. In the support materials we have included some optional reading to illustrate how children's understandings and achievements may differ. Some of this information refers to child development, and accompanying theories, in areas that link to the scale. However, we would like to stress that we do not adhere to the outdated view of child development that regards all children as developing in a uniform way and at a uniform rate related to ages and stages. Rather, we add the information for those who wish to use it to support and guide their observations, to identify individual differences, and to recognize suitable developments and adaptations to practice. These notes may also support the professional development of colleagues who have received limited training in child development.

Content of the SSTEW Scale

There are five areas of practice linked to particular aspects of development, called sub-scales. Within these are 14 subheadings called items. Within each item there are blocks of text that describe practice and are called indicators. The sub-scales and items are as follows:

1   Building trust, confidence and independence
    - Item 1: Self-regulation and social development
    - Item 2: Encouraging choices and independent play
    - Item 3: Planning for small group and individual interactions/ adult deployment

2   Social and emotional well-being
    - Item 4: Supporting socio-emotional well-being

3   Supporting and extending language and communication
    - Item 5: Encouraging children to talk with others
    - Item 6: Staff actively listen to children and encourage children to listen
    - Item 7: Staff support children's language use
    - Item 8: Sensitive responsiveness

4   Supporting learning and critical thinking
    - Item 9: Supporting curiosity and problem-solving
    - Item 10: Encouraging sustained shared thinking through storytelling, sharing books, singing, and rhymes
    - Item 11: Encouraging sustained shared thinking in investigation and exploration
    - Item 12: Supporting concept development and higher-order thinking

5   Assessing learning and language
    - Item 13: Using assessment to support and extend learning and critical thinking
    - Item 14: Assessing language development

Preparing to use the SSTEW Scale

Before using the SSTEW Scale for professional development or practice improvement, you are strongly advised to attend a SSTEW Scale training session. However, if you are using the SSTEW Scale for research purposes you *must* attend appropriate training. Even if you have attended training on other environment rating scales, many of the ideas and concepts in the SSTEW Scale are entirely new. Using the scales demands a high level of understanding not only about the content of the scale but also in making sense of what is being observed. In addition to the content of the scale, you will need to understand the paperwork found in the setting, including any planning and learning journals that are typically kept to support learning and assessment. You may need to ask non-leading questions of staff to supplement your understanding. You will therefore need to feel confident in interviewing skills and be able to respectfully, non-judgementally, and sensitively question practitioners for important information. For these reasons we suggest that it is important for assessors using the SSTEW Scale to have a good grounding in early years practice, cultural sensitivity, and child development.

Important guidance before you start

1   Typically, the SSTEW Scale should be completed during one session: a morning or afternoon of 3–4 hours in length. You should observe only one group of children at a time. All areas to which the children have access, both indoors and outside, should be observed. If you intend to observe other groups, then additional sessions will be needed.

2   We suggest that the SSTEW Scale is completed alongside one of the other ERS, and recommend ECERS-E if you are observing children in the 3–5 age range and ITERS-R if you are observing 2-year-olds. If you are also completing another ERS you will need to allow at least a further 3–4 hours, possibly longer. In addition, you will need some time at the end of the observation to talk to a member of staff who is free of early education and childcare duties and without other distractions. And you will need time to look at any relevant paperwork and then ask any additional questions.

3   Before beginning your observation, gather some background information about the setting and familiarize yourself with the layout. It may also be useful to look at any planning for the session so you are aware what activities will be available.

4   Also before you start, ensure you have completed as much of the paperwork pertaining to names, age groups etc. of the setting, and found out which staff are present and whether this is a typical day.

5   Finally, make sure you are familiar with the section below on making judgements.

Making judgements

We are expecting the scores you give to represent an overall and professional judgement of staff behaviours, responses, and interactions and the resulting children's experiences within the setting. This requires a considered response to all judgements, and these will necessarily vary according to whether the behaviours, responses, and interactions under scrutiny are positive and likely to enhance the children's learning and development, or negative and potentially harmful, as we explain below.

Making judgements with regards to potentially *positive* behaviours, responses, and interactions

Example:

Sub-scale 3: Supporting and extending children's language and communication
Item 6: Staff actively listen to children and encourage children to listen.
7.1 Staff allow long pauses, so the children have time to think and respond. They also show how they allow different lengths of pauses with different children.
7.2 Staff encourage the children to talk and listen to each other by suggesting they tell another person. Or by inviting other children to come and listen to what another child has to say or show.

In order to record a 'Yes' for these descriptions, we would expect the behaviour, response, and/or interaction to be observed at least once during the observation period. Then we would expect you to make a judgement about the potential for this to be experienced by all of the children in the setting on a regular basis – that is, to ascertain that such experiences could happen daily and potentially with all children.

This is likely to require noting which member(s) of staff were observed engaging in the interactions so that it would be possible to identify which member(s) of staff had those skills. If the skills are limited to one or two members of staff, you would then need to determine whether the member(s) of staff have access to all of the children and whether they would be available every day.

The judgements recognize the fact that some staff may be better at supporting children's learning and development than others, but also consider the setting as a whole and all of the children's experiences within it. Like many other similar ERSs, the setting could potentially achieve high scores, even though all staff are not all able to support the children in the same way.

Making judgements with regards to potentially *negative* behaviours, responses, and interactions

Example:

Sub-scale 2: Social and emotional well-being
Item 4: Supporting socio-emotional well-being
1.1 Feelings expressed by the children are played down, ignored, dismissed or ridiculed.

Here, the judgement is clear, as any observation of negative behaviour, responses, or interactions for any one child or by any one member of staff is sufficient evidence for recording it as a 'Yes'. Again, this is consistent with judgements in other similar ERSs.

Conducting an observation

1   Score an item only after you have allowed sufficient time to make a reasoned judgement – and remember, if this relates to positive practice, it might depend on whether the member(s) of staff is accessible to all children on a daily basis. You need to be sure that what you are observing is representative of the practices as a whole.

2   The items do not need to be scored in the order they appear in the book. If there is a science activity or you notice some singing or reading, you may score items relating to those first. It is often best to make notes and rate everything at the end of an observation session, but before you leave the setting.

3   There are a few items, typically at level 7, which may not to be appropriate when making observations of children who are all under the age of 3 years. These have been marked with an N/A next to them. If the group you are observing consists only of 2-year-old children, please ensure that you consider the supplementary information and mark these as N/A if appropriate.

4   Some items require you to make a judgement about 'most children' based upon what you see. 'Most children' would typically suggest more than 75 per cent. However, if you notice that one or two children appear to be consistently excluded from some activities and practices, you should not give credit for that indicator.

5   Take care not to interrupt or otherwise interfere with the practice in the setting. You should adopt a 'fly on the wall' role (non-participant observer) and avoid interacting with the staff and children if possible. It might be worth deciding what you will say to inquisitive children in advance so as not to upset them or engage them for too long. Remain as neutral and inconspicuous as possible.

6   Remember to make clear and detailed notes as you score as this may be useful for clarification and for feedback if given.

7   Before you leave the setting, make sure that you have scored all of the items. It is difficult to score items once you have left the setting. Remember to express your gratitude.

8   You may photocopy the summary of items score sheets found at the end of the booklet for use during your observations. All photocopying should be for your personal use only and all assessors should have their own original SSTEW Scale.

Scoring the SSTEW Scale

NOTE: You should start using the SSTEW Scale only once you are familiar with it, and after having read the section above: 'Important guidance before you start'.

1 Scores must reflect observed practice and not just something that the staff have told you about.

2 Some of the indicators have further information to support your judgements in the accompanying sections headed 'Examples and supplementary information' following each item. You will find a small asterisk at the end of the indicators where examples and supplementary information have been added. The information includes examples that illustrate practice, provides questions you might use, and indicates when you should consider extra paperwork, records, planning etc.

3 The SSTEW Scale scores range from 1 to 7, where 1 = inadequate, 3 = minimal, 5 = good, and 7 = excellent.

4 You should always start your observations with 1 and then systematically work through the levels.

5 A score of 1 must be given if any indicator at level 1 is scored YES.

6 A score of 2 is credited when all indicators at level 1 are marked as NO and at least half but not all of the indicators at level 3 are marked YES.

7 A score of 3 is credited when all indicators at level 1 are marked as NO and all indicators at level 3 are marked as YES.

8 A score of 4 is credited when all indicators at level 1 are marked as NO, all indicators at level 3 are marked as YES, and at least half but not all of the indicators at level 5 are marked as YES.

9 A score of 5 is credited when all indicators at level 1 are marked as NO, all indicators at level 3 are marked as YES, and all indicators at level 5 are marked as YES.

10 A score of 6 is credited when all indicators at level 1 are marked as NO, all indicators at level 3 are marked as YES, all indicators at level 5 are marked as YES, and at least half of the indicators at level 7 but not all are marked as YES.

11 A score of 7 is credited when all indicators at level 1 are marked as NO, all indicators at level 3 are marked as YES, all indicators at level 5 are marked as YES, and all indicators at level 7 are marked as YES.

12 To calculate the average score for the sub-scale you need to add up all of the ratings for the individual items and then divide by the number of items scored.

13 The total mean score for the SSTEW Scale is the sum of all of the item ratings divided by the total number of items scored (14).

The SSTEW Scale score sheet, profile, and joint observation sheets

A separate score sheet is available for you to photocopy at the end of the book (page 40). It makes interpretation of the scores much easier when it is possible to view them together.

The SSTEW Scale profile on page 47 allows you to present your scores in a visual format, which should support the detection of patterns of practice, including identifying any strengths and/or areas for improvement. The SSTEW Scale profile allows you to plot **three** sets of observations. This can be useful to show differences between assessors and/or show progress over time. If you plot the scores using different-coloured ink (or otherwise indicating difference), you should potentially see progress over time (if the observations are taken at different times) or different scores (if the observations are made by different assessors).

The joint observation sheet (page 59) is designed to support discussion between different assessors and to illustrate a final agreed score. When observations are undertaken by more than one assessor in the same centre, such as during training and/or to ensure inter-rater reliability, typically the observers will set aside a time at the end of their observations to discuss and agree their scores. The agreed score may be an average of the observers' original scores, but more typically one observer has seen some practice that is important and has been missed by the other observer(s). All of the observers give evidence to support their scores and after discussion a final score is agreed (which may be the original score of one observer).

Sub-scale 1. Building trust, confidence and independence

Item 1. Self-regulation and social development

Inadequate		Minimal		Good		Excellent
1	2	3	4	5	6	7

Inadequate — 1

1.1 Staff do not appear to agree about the boundaries/rules/expectations or apply them consistently.*

1.2 Some children are left, even though they are obviously confused or distressed.

Minimal — 3

3.1 Expectations and boundaries are made explicit and shared by all staff.*

3.2 Staff are respectful and professional around the children, parents/carers, and each other.*

Good — 5

5.1 Staff explain carefully to the children what they need to do and pre-empt any difficulties.*

5.2 Staff show empathy and understanding when children do not want to follow rules or get upset.*

5.3 Staff show an awareness of individuals and their needs, giving additional support and allowing some flexibility.*

5.4 Staff redirect inappropriate behaviour by stating what the children should do rather than what they should not.

Excellent — 7

7.1 Staff congratulate children when they follow the rules well – e.g. I saw you help put the tractor away. And/or the children are encouraged to tell staff how they followed the rules etc.*

7.2 Staff have agreed processes that they follow when conflicts arise. The processes include engaging the children in problem-solving and finding solutions to disputes together.*

Examples and supplementary information

1.1 Nothing appears to be written or agreed about behaviour. Examples include seeing staff respond differently to children and giving them different messages about noise level, running, sharing, and the numbers of children allowed in different areas or the time allowed to use different resources.

3.1 Staff give children the same messages. Some rules may be illustrated in the setting/classroom, e.g. two chairs available, pictures of two children to denote that two children are allowed in an area, photos of children with overalls on in the painting area, wellington boots positioned by the door to outside etc.

3.2 Staff are polite to everyone and listen well. They talk about work-related matters and keep personal discussions to a minimum unless related to supporting children to learn.

5.1 Staff are heard explaining simple rules and expectations in positive terms to the children, e.g. remember to share the bikes; remember to listen to each other; I can hear you so you don't need to shout/yell. They may have agreed signals to support organization, e.g. a tidy-up song, a handclap, or a short game of Simon Says to gain attention. They may show support to some children more by their presence, help etc.

5.2 Staff show an appreciation of and verbalize the children's feelings when upset, angry, tired, happy, e.g. I can see you are angry; yes, I understand that you wanted that; I can see you are feeling happy.

5.3 Staff support appropriate behaviour according to a child's needs, e.g. by modelling appropriate behaviour, giving individual instructions, prompts, and support, allowing extra time, putting activities somewhere safe for the child to return to later or verbally if older, e.g. asking children to talk quietly, play together, share.

7.1 This may happen on an individual basis or during small group time.

7.2 Staff need to understand and follow a conflict resolution process – actively seeing child-to-child conflict as a potential learning situation. They may follow something like HighScope's six steps to conflict resolution (see page 51) or Peaceful Problem-Solving (PPS). They will probably need some sort of prompts to support all staff following this. If no conflict is witnessed, ask a non-leading **Question:** What do you typically do when the children get into arguments, fights, or other conflicts? Prompt: Do all the staff do the same? Do you have an agreed protocol?

Sub-scale 1. Building trust, confidence and independence

Item 2. Encouraging choices and independent play

Inadequate		Minimal		Good		Excellent
1	2	3	4	5	6	7

1.1 The interests of the children are not taken into account when planning the session.

1.2 Staff do not allow children to act independently.

3.1 Staff 'step back' from the children's play; they do not interfere unnecessarily. The theme, level of complexity, aim, choice of play is accepted.

3.2 Books, toys, resources are easily accessible to the children and staff accept and welcome that the children may use equipment/resources in a different way from their intended purpose and may rearrange the furniture.

3.3 It is accepted that some children may wish to undertake a different activity from the rest of the group.*

3.4 The schedule/routine is flexible enough to allow for individual interests, and free choice/play is an everyday occurrence.

5.1 If invited, the staff will join in with the children's play while allowing the children to lead, respecting the level of play and rules established by the children.*

5.2 Staff show enjoyment and a sense of fun when watching or joining in with children's play. They will set up new activities if the children ask.*

5.3 While the children's play is respected, the children are, nonetheless, expected to remain within the boundaries/rules of the setting.*

5.4 Staff provide the necessary resources to enrich and support play, according to the suggestions given by the children.*

7.1 Staff include children in planning for the setting, e.g. consulting parents/carers, supporting children in choosing and making props for play areas, mind mapping, deciding whether to make a visit or have a visitor etc.

7.2 Staff observe the children following their adult-supported activities to see if any of the ideas, concepts etc. from these are incorporated in their free play.*

Examples and supplementary information

3.3 This item is about acceptance and acknowledging that children may want to do a different activity from the rest of the group. On most occasions, this is accepted and allowed, especially with the youngest children and during play or activities. However, there will be times when this is not possible or desirable, in which case the adults clearly show that they understand and respect the child's wishes while redirecting them in a gentle, supportive, and calm way. For example, 'I can see that you do not want to go but Daddy is waiting, let's put your model somewhere safe for you to continue tomorrow.'

5.1 If not seen, then ask **Question:** Do the children ever ask you or other members of staff to join their play? If not, then it is probably because they do not make good playmates and mark 'No'. If yes, ask **Question:** How does that go, can you give an example?

5.2 This indicator reflects both the staff showing a sense of fun/enjoyment as well as responsiveness. While you do not need to see the staff setting up a new activity for the children if they do not ask for it, you could ask **Question:** What do you do if the children ask for different activities/resources from those set out? And/or make a judgement based on the staff's responsiveness to children during play, other activities, and routines within the setting.

5.3 You see clear evidence of the children following the setting/classroom rules or alternatively being gently reminded of them.

5.4 If not seen, then ask **Questions:** How do you decide what to put out for the children? Do the children ever ask for more/different resources? If so, how do you respond?

7.2 Look at the **observations, records, and planning** sheets to see if the children have the opportunity to, and then have chosen to, incorporate ideas, resources, roles, vocabulary learnt earlier in their free play (e.g. choose to be characters from previous day's book they had read, choose to use resources from an adult-supported session, play in role-play area copying previously modelled role by adult).

Sub-scale 1. Building trust, confidence and independence

Item 3. Planning for small group and individual interactions/adult deployment

Inadequate		Minimal		Good		Excellent
1	2	3	4	5	6	7
1.1 Staff show little understanding that groups and groupings are important.*		3.1 The setting is arranged with enough choice so that children can play alone, in pairs, in small groups.		5.1 Children are involved in making choices about areas/ spaces and resources.*		7.1 Planning is flexible to the needs of the children. It can change to follow the sudden interests of the children and/ or activities are abandoned if no one wants to do them.*
1.2 No clear delineation of areas for groups or schedule to allow for group and individual time.		3.2 Staff ensure that individual areas within the setting do not become overcrowded, e.g. pictures and/or number labels are used to support older children's understanding of number limits in specific areas.		5.2 Staff position themselves in areas so that they can see the whole area but also so that they can work with small groups/individuals.		7.2 Staff spend their time scaffolding learning across the setting and concentrate on the children they are working with while doing this. They are, however, also aware of and responsive to the rest of the children.
				5.3 Spaces are monitored regularly to ensure there are sufficient spaces/resources in popular areas and to remake, and then support children to interact with, previously unpopular areas.*		7.3 Staff engage in activities specifically designed to encourage children to come and see what they are doing. This is to engage in individual and small group interactions and/or discussions.*

Examples and supplementary information

3.3 No evidence of grouping children can be seen throughout the observed period and none can be seen on **planning or other paperwork**.

5.1 If not seen, ask **Question:** How do you decide on the areas in the setting and what should go in them?

5.3 If not seen, ask **Questions:** How do you monitor the use of different areas in the setting? What do you do if you find that an area has become unpopular?

7.1 If not seen through changes revolving around the children and activities abandoned, ask **Question:** What do you do if the children do not seem interested in the play routines or the activities on offer?

7.3 This is about signalling availability of staff to the children. Some staff sit in an area that has space for children to join them and complete activities that might interest the children but which show the children that they are available to chat should they wish to join them, e.g. sorting buttons, small world toys, folding paper etc.

Sub-scale 2. Social and emotional well-being

Item 4. Supporting socio-emotional well-being

	Inadequate		Minimal		Good		Excellent
	1	2	3	4	5	6	7

Inadequate — 1

1.1 Feelings expressed by the children are played down, ignored, dismissed or ridiculed.

1.2 Staff do not display a warm and welcoming body language to the children.

1.3 Staff do not lay out the setting or organize activities to encourage social interaction.*

Minimal — 3

3.1 Staff empathize with the children and help them to deal with feelings expressed.*

3.2 Staff encourage children to play alongside each other, providing additional toys/props and resources to support continued play. As the children progress to playing together, staff support them in helping each other and sharing.

3.3 Positive individual attention is paid to most children at some point during the session.*

3.4 Staff are warm, friendly, and calm. They use calming gestures, physical proximity, pats, and hugs when necessary and appropriate.

Good — 5

5.1 Children are encouraged to express/say what they feel and need.*

5.2 Planning shows evidence of learning intentions that are designed to support social interaction, including encouraging collaborative activities and play where appropriate.*

5.3 Children are encouraged to seek an adult's support when sharing or playing breaks down.*

5.4 Staff are responsive to the children's needs, feelings, and moods. They may play, show liveliness, and have fun with the children, supporting positive emotions.*

Excellent — 7

7.1 Staff provide opportunities for children to talk about feelings and needs – often using the children's own experiences. They may use stories or props, e.g. 'puppet misses his family, how shall we make him feel better?'

7.2 Children are asked to show or say what they can understand from the non-verbal expressions of others in the group, from story books, photos, DVDs etc.*

7.3 Staff support children in communicating with, and recognizing and responding to the feelings of others, including where children may have difficulty expressing their needs or wants.*

7.4 Staff look beyond the children to explain their feelings, making changes within the environment/routine etc. when necessary.*

Examples and supplementary information

1.3 Consider the resources and their positioning. Are there several similar resources set out in enclosed and safe spaces? Do the staff encourage children to play together? Are there cosy quiet areas and role-play areas?

3.1 Staff identify the children's emotions and feelings (e.g. tired, happy, angry, sad, frightened, hungry, hot, cold) and support them calmly and respectfully.

3.3 'Most children' equates to 75 per cent. However, if any one child or children are consistently ignored or paid only negative attention, do not give credit here.

5.1 Staff ask children how they feel/what they need as appropriate. They offer alternatives/possible solutions for children to choose/indicate what they need. For those children who need it, the staff interpret and verbalize feelings for them, ensuring a proportionate 'half and half' mix of positive and negative feelings/emotions.

5.2 Examples: staff member A supports and encourages child B to allow child C to join her/his play; includes resource X in area A so that children X, Y, and Z can resume and continue their game of last week.

5.3 If not seen either by staff as they talk through conflicts or by the children asking for support or otherwise indicating their need for support by looking at adults/verbalizing etc. with obvious intention, ask **Question:** How do you support children in seeking adult support when sharing or playing breaks down?

5.4 The key word here is 'responsiveness' and when appropriate, support for positive emotions through play, a sense of fun, and enjoyment. Staff show they understand how emotions can be 'catching'. **Question:** Why is having fun and showing enjoyment important?

7.2 Depending on the age and understanding of the children, this may involve adult-supported activities using resources such as photos, books, DVDs, and/or responding to incidental happenings in the setting. Again, depending on the children's abilities, this may include discussion, naming emotions, and making links to their own experiences or more physical responses such as gentle pats, big smiles, hugs etc.

7.3 Staff point out other children's feelings and engage in 'discussions' with other children to develop empathy and appropriate responses. They interpret and verbalize children's needs and feelings to others to support communication and encourage collaboration. If not seen, ask **Questions:** How might you support a child who wanted to join in with the play of others but was unable to express this? How might you support children to share and play together?

7.4 If no evidence is seen, ask **Questions:** What do you do if you notice a change in a child's behaviour in the setting? What do you think is likely to affect a child's behaviour in the setting?

Sub-scale 3. Supporting and extending language and communication

Item 5. Encouraging children to talk with others

Inadequate		Minimal		Good		Excellent
1	2	3	4	5	6	7

1

1.1 Children are discouraged from speaking more than is necessary.

1.2 Staff talk to children primarily to change their behaviour and to manage routines.

1.3 The noise levels within the setting are not conducive to talk, e.g. too noisy due to music or songs being piped into the setting.

3

3.1 Children are allowed to speak whenever possible.

3.2 Staff attempt to engage in conversations with most children within the group.*

5

5.1 Children are encouraged to talk to each other during activities and throughout the day. The staff model and support this.

5.2 During adult-guided activities the children are given resources (etc.) that support, and are grouped to support, talk.*

5.3 Staff ensure that each child who wants to speak has the opportunity to do so. They interact with individuals and small groups to support this.

5.4 Where children are reticent or unable to talk and/or have English as an additional language, alternative methods of communication are employed, e.g. photographs, pictures, symbols, puppets, gestures, tape recordings from home.*

7

7.1 Children are encouraged to choose and lead interactions, conversations, and/or play.

7.2 Children are encouraged to take more turns in an interaction, possibly giving longer and more complex answers as staff allow for this by increasing their waiting time, adding comments, and asking simple questions.

7.3 Where children are reticent about interacting with others, staff play alongside the children, taking cues from them and following their lead, waiting to be invited to communicate.*

7.4 Staff provide running commentaries of individuals' and/or small groups' actions etc. to support longer play and interactions with other children.*

Examples and supplementary information

3.2 'Most children' equates to 75 per cent. However, if there are some children who appear to be deliberately avoided, do not give credit here.

5.2 If not seen, ask **Questions:** Are children grouped for adult-guided activities? If yes, how are the groupings chosen?

5.4 Note: Include Makaton here, especially if used across the setting with all children. If not seen, ask **Questions:** How do you support play, communication, and talk with children who are reticent to talk or who have English as an additional language?

7.3 If not seen, ask **Question:** What do you do to support communication and talk with children who are reticent to talk or who have EAL? (NB: You may have already asked this for 5.4.)

7.4 If not seen, ask **Question:** How might you support children with little vocabulary, fewer language skills, or a reticence to play and interact with other children to do so?

Sub-scale 3. Supporting and extending language and communication

Item 6. Staff actively listen to children and encourage children to listen

Inadequate		Minimal		Good		Excellent
1	2	3	4	5	6	7
1.1 Staff stifle communication by, e.g. being judgemental or by humiliating, ignoring or belittling the children. 1.2 Requests for help are ignored (*whether the requests be direct or indirect, e.g. crying, withdrawal, inactivity*).		3.1 Children's verbal messages are understood. 3.2 Staff respond to verbal and non-verbal signs from children. 3.3 The body language of the staff shows that they want to communicate (*open arms, inclined head, smiles, waiting and listening*).		5.1 Staff position themselves at the children's height when talking or listening to them. 5.2 Rephrasing and/or repeating is used to check that the children have been understood. 5.3 Where meaning or speech is unclear, staff make an 'educated guess' rather than asking the child to constantly repeat her/himself. Then, if they have guessed wrongly, staff take the blame for it.*		7.1 Staff allow long pauses, so the children have time to think and respond. They also show how they allow different lengths of pauses with different children.* 7.2 Staff encourage the children to talk and listen to each other by suggesting they tell another person. Or by inviting other children to come and listen to what another child has to say or show.*

Examples and supplementary information

5.3 If not seen, ask **Questions:** How do you manage children with unclear speech? What do you do if you really do not understand what they are saying?

7.1 If not seen, ask **Question:** How do you and other staff ensure that children have enough time to think before responding to questions?

7.2 Examples may be encouraging children to show and talk about models, paintings, resources, props, ideas, collaborate in play etc. with each other. For younger children, the talk may be limited to labelling what they show while older children might explain processes and engage in positive evaluations.

Sub-scale 3: Supporting and extending language and communication

Item 7. Staff support children's language use

Inadequate		Minimal		Good		Excellent
1	2	3	4	5	6	7

Inadequate — 1

1.1 Children are often spoken to in a 'babyish' way *(mimicking the way young children speak).*

1.2 Staff often use poor or inappropriate language.*

1.3 Staff often use language that the children do not understand.

Minimal — 3

3.1 Staff employ simple and correct language with the correct use of grammar and pronunciation.

3.2 Staff use a tone of voice appropriate to the need and situation.

3.3 The level of language is appropriate to the age and ability of the children.

Good — 5

5.1 Staff show care in the choice of correct and appropriate terms.

5.2 Staff use varied tones of voice to support interest, excitement, express emotions, calm children, and support understanding.

5.3 Staff provide running commentaries to model vocabulary and to display their own thought processes for children while they play.

Excellent — 7

7.1 Staff support language development on an individual level by using correct forms of incorrect words, phrases, and grammar during interactions with the children. They do not point out the child's mistake – they just model the correct word, sentence etc.

7.2 The staff scaffold and model language with individual children that is slightly above the child's current level.*

Examples and supplementary information

1.2 Staff may use grammatically incorrect sentences, childish and inappropriate words, and/or slang.

7.2 Examples of typical language development can be found in Table 3 on page 53. This may be useful when making judgements on language that is slightly above the individual child's current level.

Sub-scale 3. Supporting and extending language and communication

Item 8. Sensitive responsiveness

Inadequate		Minimal		Good		Excellent
1	2	3	4	5	6	7
1.1 Little effort is made to engage with the children (e.g. in conversation, to show any interest in what the children are doing etc.).		3.1 Staff focus on small groups of children and respond to individuals within the group.		5.1 Staff ensure that most children receive extended individual attention at least once during the session.*		7.1 Most children are given one-on-one interactive attention more than once during the session.*
1.2 Staff often talk among themselves and ignore the children in front of them.		3.2 Staff listen out for and respond to any questions or comments from children in an interested way.		5.2 Help is willingly offered if the staff feel that children may be struggling with the task in hand.		7.2 Any comments or requests from children are responded to or dealt with promptly – if necessary, involving another member of staff to ensure that children are not left waiting and wondering.*
1.3 Little effort is made to treat the children as individuals. Instead, children are communicated with en masse (as a group) at all times.		3.3 Praise is used, but indiscriminately and generally to the whole group.		5.3 Praise and encouragement are readily given to individuals when appropriate.		7.3 Although staff members may wish to focus on an individual child, no other child in the group is made to feel excluded.
1.4 Children are left in obvious distress.						

Examples and supplementary information

5.1 'Most children' equates to 75 per cent. However, if one child or more appear to be consistently ignored, do not give credit here.

7.1 If not seen, ask **Question:** How do you ensure that all of the children are happy and learning? **Prompt:** Do you have a system that you use to ensure every child is happy? Do you know if every/most child(ren) in the setting has/have an opportunity to interact with an adult individually during sessions?

7.2 This refers to responses and supporting language and communication and so is more about extending and supporting activities and play than following conflicts, distress etc., which are covered in Sub-scale 1: Building trust and confidence.

Sub-scale 4. Supporting learning and critical thinking

Item 9. Supporting curiosity and problem-solving

Inadequate		Minimal		Good		Excellent
1	2	3	4	5	6	7

1

1.1 The learning environment is always set out in the same way and includes the same resources and activities.

1.2 Staff stand back and allow the children to play by themselves all of the time unless there is conflict.

3

3.1 There are a variety of resources available at each session. Activities/play routines are chosen that the adults know the children will want to undertake.

3.2 Staff offer at least one adult-supported activity during a session.*

3.3 Staff ask children to help them solve problems – e.g. while setting up areas, the children find and help them put out resources.

5

5.1 New resources, activities, or challenges are set up regularly. They are linked to the current theme or time of year or children's interests or schemas.*

5.2 Staff model, support, and extend children's learning in ALL areas of the setting, moving from one area to the next as appropriate.*

5.3 Staff challenge and support problem-solving – e.g. by posing small everyday problems or inviting children to solve problems as they arise.

7

7.1 Planning shows there have been regular visitors, e.g. police, local shopkeepers, taxi drivers, and/or staff dressed as characters in familiar stories playing a role.

7.2 Visits are made to places of interest and/or to extend children's knowledge and experiences.*

7.3 Staff support curiosity by hiding unexpected objects and/or using treasure boxes to be discovered during play.*

7.4 Staff support children's metacognition by talking aloud to model their thinking and problem-solving processes and support children to plan, undertake, and then review activities.*

Examples and supplementary information

3.2 Take a 'session' as a morning or afternoon.

5.1 If not obvious through observation, **planning**, or other information, ask **Question:** How do you decide which activities to plan and set out for the children?

5.2 If not obvious through observation, **planning**, or other information, ask **Question:** How do you decide on the adult's role in relation to the play and areas in the setting?

7.2 If not obvious through **planning and photographs** etc., ask **Questions:** Do you take the children out on trips? How do you decide where to go and what to do? Do you plan any follow-up activities? Can you provide an example?

7.3 This is about supporting children's wish to discover and engage in discussion/problem-solving through introducing surprises and unexpected artefacts in the environment for them to discover (e.g. in the garden, an unidentified object such as an engine part, crystals, fossils, toys in sandpit, treasure boxes). Staff then support their wonder and problem-solving. If not obvious through observation, **planning and photographs** etc., ask **Questions:** How do you encourage curiosity in the children? Do you introduce surprises and things for the children to find and discover within the setting? Can you provide an example?

7.4 With younger children this could involve staff modelling feeling states and empathizing with others. With older children it might include conversations about thoughts, wishes, and feelings. They may use 'I wonder ...' statements and questions; they may explain how they are planning to do things, how things went, and what they might do differently. With children who are capable of evaluation, they may support them, reviewing their activities, play, and any outcomes/products etc.

Sub-scale 4. Supporting learning and critical thinking

Item 10. Encouraging sustained shared thinking through storytelling, sharing books, singing, and rhymes

Inadequate		Minimal		Good		Excellent
1	2	3	4	5	6	7

Inadequate (1)	Minimal (3)	Good (5)	Excellent (7)
1.1 Very little individual interaction during story/book time, singing, or rhymes.	3.1 Staff respond to children asking for stories, books, singing, or rhymes by helping them recall stories, locate and read books, singing with or engaging in rhyming, and word play as appropriate.	5.1 Staff encourage the children to hold and 'read' books or retell familiar stories, including their own 'stories', sing songs, or join in with rhymes and word games.	7.1 Staff use factual books to support children's understanding of concepts.*
1.2 Staff involvement with stories, books, singing, or rhymes is limited to whole group time.	3.2 Staff invite children (individually or in small groups) to join them to sing, engage in word and rhyme play, or tell stories or read books.	5.2 Staff use props/puppets/ the children themselves to support storytelling, engagement with songs or rhymes.	7.2 Staff engage children with stories, singing etc. They support anticipation of familiar words, actions etc., make comments, evaluate stories/songs etc., and ask a few simple open-ended questions.*
	3.3 Staff engage children in choosing songs, rhymes, stories, or books and ask them about their choices.	5.3 Children are given access to props and puppets to support retelling stories and use in free play.	7.3 Staff encourage children to make links between the story, book, song, or rhyme and their previous experiences.
	3.4 Staff show that they know the children's preferred books, stories, songs, or rhymes.*	5.4 Staff sing and engage in rhyming and word play while playing and interacting with the children during other activities.	

Examples and supplementary information

3.4 If not seen, ask **Questions:** How do you decide which songs/rhymes/books/stories to choose? Do any of the children have favourites? How do you know about those?

7.1 Evidence might include finding factual books in areas of the setting other than the book corner as well as staff bringing them to the attention of children during discussions.

7.2 Evidence for this might include staff leaving gaps in their singing, reading etc. Simple questions may vary depending on the children's abilities and experiences. For example, they may be about simple recall and order of events or where appropriate more complex, e.g. discussing different meanings of words (especially when words have alternative meanings), asking about the story from the different characters' viewpoints, inviting children to make up alternative endings, asking what if, why, and how questions.

Sub-scale 4. Supporting learning and critical thinking

Item 11. Encouraging sustained shared thinking in investigation and exploration

Inadequate		Minimal		Good		Excellent
1	2	3	4	5	6	7

1

1.1 Very little exploration and investigation is encouraged.

1.2 Staff show little understanding of science/maths/problem-solving or concepts.*

3

3.1 Staff set out activities and open-ended resources deliberately to encourage exploration.

3.2 Staff discuss children's explorations and investigations with them.

3.3 Staff encourage children to make connections between what they observe and their previous experiences or with follow-up activities. They make use of pictures (e.g. in books or on the computer) and other resources to support this.

5

5.1 Staff encourage the children to use their imagination and creativity to explore and experiment. They encourage children to bring resources/scientific equipment from area to area.*

5.2 Staff model exploration, excitement, and wonder for children to watch and then engage with.

5.3 Staff point out, share, and explain the actions and interests of the children as they occur. They introduce simple scientific and explanatory concepts.*

5.4 Science/maths activities are organized so that they build upon previous activities and explorations.*

7

7.1 Staff model using scientific/problem-solving approaches for the children to watch. They support careful watching, prediction, anticipation, and evaluation through talk and action.

7.2 Staff use scientific words, e.g. 'dissolve', linking these to the children's experiences, as well as to more familiar ideas as they occur.* *N/A permitted: see supplementary information.*

7.3 Staff talk about and encourage parents/carers to join in with their children's scientific/problem-solving activities and explorations.

Examples and supplementary information

1.2 During activities where these ideas and concepts could be explored, opportunities for this are ignored – e.g. during cake-making no mention of melting, liquids, and solids and/or changes that are seen during heating/cooling or mixing, etc.

5.1 Staff encourage children to play with resources in an exploratory way, e.g. mixing paint to look at colour change rather than painting, freezing small toys in ice to discover and talk about melting. They encourage children to use scientific and maths resources in their play, e.g. pipettes, magnifying glasses etc.

5.3 Examples might include discussion of different textures and surfaces and how they affect play and movement, e.g. rough textures slow down the ball and bike, the smooth slide helps to make you go fast. Other examples might be: it is loud because it is close, it looks small because it is far away, and pointing out shadows, animals, insects, and how plants move and grow etc.

5.4 Progression should be evident in **planning and other records or assessments**.

7.2 Staff link scientific ideas to experiences, e.g. while playing with magnets, introduce the words 'attract' and 'repel'; while cooking, introduce 'melting', 'liquid', 'solid'; while using forces when playing outside, for instance, introduce the words 'push' and 'pull' so that the children have direct experience of these ideas and concepts as they are discussed. Then also make links to familiar ideas and concepts: it is melting like your ice cream does on a hot day, the magnet attracts like a big hug and repels like a push down a slide, or the wind is blowing you away.

7.2 continued **Re N/A permitted:** When observing children under 3 years old, particularly if they are only just 2 and/or have very limited language skills, please use your judgement as to whether introducing scientific language such as 'dissolve' is appropriate. In most instances, we believe enriching the children's language in this way is appropriate and where this is not present it represents a missed opportunity. However, we also recognize that in certain circumstances this may confuse children who are just learning to talk. You may find Table 3 on page 53 useful to support your decision. If you do choose N/A, please note your reasoning next to the score sheet.

Sub-scale 4. Supporting learning and critical thinking

Item 12. Supporting children's concept development and higher-order thinking

Inadequate		Minimal		Good		Excellent
1	2	3	4	5	6	7
1.1 Staff do not appear to plan to support children's thinking and concept development.		3.1 Staff set up resources and run adult-guided sessions that support children to think critically, such as sequencing, comparing, contrasting, and problem-solving. 3.2 When children ask for help they get support in finding their own solutions to their queries.		5.1 Staff support the children in thinking through what they are doing and extending it through modelling, asking simple open and closed questions, and providing additional resources. 5.2 Planning shows evidence of learning intentions that lead to activities and questions designed to support or extend thinking and problem-solving.		7.1 Children are encouraged to plan for their own learning. Adults may help them to gather materials, resources, produce 'lists', use photos, brainstorm, or mind map ready for an activity. 7.2 Children are encouraged to evaluate their activities and play through adult questioning.* *N/A permitted: see supplementary information.* 7.3 Planning shows progression and provides children with the opportunities to develop concepts they have explored previously, e.g. through schemas, interests.* 7.4 Children are supported to see how the concepts they are exploring link to real life and their existing experiences, e.g. through visits, photos, discussion with parents/carers.*

Examples and supplementary information

7.2 **Re N/A permitted:** When observing children under 3 years old, particularly if they are only just 2 and/or have very limited language skills, please use your judgement as to whether introducing the idea of evaluation is appropriate. In most instances we believe that it is possible to listen to children in such a way as to support their development of evaluation and where this is not present it represents a missed opportunity. However, we also recognize that in certain circumstances this may not be possible. If you do choose N/A, please note your reasoning next to the score sheet.

7.3 **Planning** should show this progression.

7.4 **Planning and other records**, e.g. learning journeys should show this.

Sub-scale 5. Assessing learning and language

Item 13. Using assessment to support and extend learning and critical thinking

Inadequate		Minimal		Good		Excellent
1	2	3	4	5	6	7

1

1.1 Assessment is conducted only to show end of stage or activity progress.

1.2 Assessment is limited to noting milestones in development.

3

3.1 Staff assess children, making links to their ongoing development.*

3.2 Staff use assessment to show progress to the parents/carers and to support smooth transitions.*

3.3 Children are assessed to alert staff to any learning and/or behaviour difficulties.*

5

5.1 Staff use assessment to inform future practice, plan adult-guided activities and materials/resources within the environment.*

5.2 Staff share simple learning objectives with the children during adult-supported activities and check whether these are achieved.*

5.3 Staff constantly assess children's engagement with activities and change activities/resources/areas depending on their use.

7

7.1 Staff observe, give children feedback, ask open-ended questions, and make suggestions.

7.2 Staff highlight successes and difficulties without being judgemental. For example, they give feedback that helps the children know what they are doing well and recognizes their strengths in the learning process. They give feedback that encourages positive learning dispositions such as persistence, concentration, and completion.*

7.3 Staff encourage children to give simple, positive, supportive feedback to one another.* *N/A permitted: see supplementary information.*

Examples and supplementary information

3.1 Links at this level are typically made to the current framework curriculum used in the setting, and are unlikely to include links to more theoretical understandings, as outlined in the Support material on pages 48–58.

3.2 Evidence of sharing assessments with parent/carers and any setting to which the child moves may be found in **paperwork**. If not seen, than ask **Questions:** What do you share with parents/carers about their child's learning and progress? What information, if any, do you pass on to any new setting/school to which a child transfers?

3.3 **Assessment, records, and paperwork** should show evidence of consideration of each child's developmental level and appropriate action if concerns are raised.

5.1 **Planning should clearly relate to assessments** and then be evident in practice on the day of observation, unless reasons for a diversion from the planning are given.

5.2 Where appropriate, the staff share simple learning objectives with the children, e g. today we are going to learn how to make chocolate cake/to play together; I can see that you are learning about magnets; oh yes, I wonder what we can find in the garden; oh, you are balancing on the logs ...

7.2 Where appropriate, staff highlight successes and frustrations and give feedback through body language and verbal expressions, suggesting surprise, interest, and delight etc. or through discussion – e.g. I saw you playing on the climbing logs, you balanced really well and tried again even though you fell off twice. Then you concentrated really hard and you managed to get across them all. How did that make you feel?

7.3 **Re N/A permitted:** When observing children under 3 years old, particularly if they are only just 2 and/or have very limited language and socio-emotional skills, please use your judgement as to whether introducing peer feedback is appropriate. If you do choose N/A, please note your reasoning next to the score sheet.

Sub-scale 5. Assessing learning and language

Item 14. Assessing language development

Inadequate		Minimal		Good		Excellent
1	2	3	4	5	6	7
1.1 Staff rarely engage in observations designed to specifically monitor and assess children's language development.		3.1 Staff assess children's language development with all other areas of learning and make simple links to development.*		5.1 Staff observe children's language, taking short word-for-word samples of children's language during interactions with adults and peers across the setting.*		7.1 Staff recognize that supporting children's play is effective in supporting language development. They observe the effect of scaffolding children's learning and supporting them to engage in more interaction with others and more complex imaginative play.*
		3.2 Staff involve parents in any assessments they make in connection to children's language development.		5.2 Staff assess and monitor children's language development, considering expressive language, comprehension, and how they use language to share meaning with others.*		7.2 Staff share their assessments and understandings with parents/carers and support them in playing with the children at home to support their development.*
		3.3 Children are assessed to alert staff to any language development difficulties, then their progress is closely monitored.*		5.3 Staff show an awareness that language may vary across different contexts, e.g. home and setting, different areas within the setting, with different members of staff, and with different play opportunities.*		

Examples and supplementary information

3.1 If not seen, then ask **Question:** How do you know what progress children are making in their language development?

3.3 If not seen, then ask **Questions:** When you are concerned about a child's language development, what do you do? How do you use the information you have about a child's language progress? Can you give me an example?

5.1 You would need to see evidence of this in the **observations** made by staff.

5.2 **Assessment techniques** and **planning** for extension and support should show that the staff understand the different aspects of language. Assessment will include discussion of children's comprehension of language, their spoken language abilities, and feedback on how they use their language to engage in play and activities with others. Their planning may include vocabulary and example questions they will use in adult-supported activities, and also while supporting child-initiated play, possibly linked to individual children. They may agree to use a consistent set of words and gestures/Makaton across the setting to support language development. Where children have identified difficulties, they will show how they appreciate the links between comprehension and spoken language/expression by planning for play with an adult to develop comprehension and avoid causing the children additional frustration – for example, by asking them to continually repeat words, phrases etc. or using overly formal approaches. They will include aspects of outside professional advice, e.g. a speech and language therapist in individual play plans for children.

5.3 **Assessment and feedback techniques** and **planning** shows that staff understand how context can impact on language and may include notes in relation to child's preferred place, person to chat with, what parents report.

7.1 If not seen during observation, should be evident in **planning, group planning, and individual plans** if needed. (The support materials on pages 48–58 may support understanding of how play links to language development.)

7.2 If not evident in **paperwork and planning**, ask **Question:** How do you include parents in the children's achievements and your plans to support them?

SSTEW Scale score sheet

Name of setting/centre _____

Date of visit _____ Time of visit: from _____ to _____

Area(s) observed in the setting/centre

_____

_____

Practitioners/teachers present

_____

_____

Age of children observed (range and average age) _____

Number of children observed on day _____ Total number of children in observed group _____

Total number of children who attend the setting/centre _____

Other pertinent information, e.g. catchment area

_____

_____

_____

Observer's name _____

Signature _____

Rough plan of indoor and outdoor areas being observed

Score sheets

Sub-scale 1   Building trust, confidence and independence

Item 1   Self-regulation and social development   1   2   3   4   5   6   7

	Y	N			Y	N			Y	N			Y	N
1.1	☐	☐		3.1	☐	☐		5.1	☐	☐		7.1	☐	☐
1.2	☐	☐		3.2	☐	☐		5.2	☐	☐		7.2	☐	☐
								5.3	☐	☐				
								5.4	☐	☐				

Sub-scale 1   Building trust, confidence and independence

Item 2   Encouraging choices and independent play   1   2   3   4   5   6   7

	Y	N			Y	N			Y	N			Y	N
1.1	☐	☐		3.1	☐	☐		5.1	☐	☐		7.1	☐	☐
1.2	☐	☐		3.2	☐	☐		5.2	☐	☐		7.2	☐	☐
				3.3	☐	☐		5.3	☐	☐				
				3.4	☐	☐		5.4	☐	☐				

Sub-scale 1   Building trust, confidence and independence

Item 3   Planning for small group and individual interactions/adult deployment   1   2   3   4   5   6   7

	Y	N			Y	N			Y	N			Y	N
1.1	☐	☐		3.1	☐	☐		5.1	☐	☐		7.1	☐	☐
1.2	☐	☐		3.2	☐	☐		5.2	☐	☐		7.2	☐	☐
								5.3	☐	☐		7.3	☐	☐

Sub-scale 2   Social and emotional well-being

Item 4   Supporting socio-emotional well-being   1   2   3   4   5   6   7

	Y	N			Y	N			Y	N			Y	N
1.1	☐	☐		3.1	☐	☐		5.1	☐	☐		7.1	☐	☐
1.2	☐	☐		3.2	☐	☐		5.2	☐	☐		7.2	☐	☐
1.3	☐	☐		3.3	☐	☐		5.3	☐	☐		7.3	☐	☐
				3.4	☐	☐		5.4	☐	☐		7.4	☐	☐

Sub-scale 3   Supporting and extending language and communication

Item 5   Encouraging children to talk with others   1   2   3   4   5   6   7

	Y	N			Y	N			Y	N			Y	N
1.1	☐	☐		3.1	☐	☐		5.1	☐	☐		7.1	☐	☐
1.2	☐	☐		3.2	☐	☐		5.2	☐	☐		7.2	☐	☐
1.3	☐	☐						5.3	☐	☐		7.3	☐	☐
								5.4	☐	☐		7.4	☐	☐

Sub-scale 3 Supporting and extending language and communication

Item 6 Staff actively listen to children and encourage children to listen

1 2 3 4 5 6 7

	Y	N		Y	N		Y	N		Y	N
1.1	☐	☐	3.1	☐	☐	5.1	☐	☐	7.1	☐	☐
1.2	☐	☐	3.2	☐	☐	5.2	☐	☐	7.2	☐	☐
			3.3	☐	☐	5.3	☐	☐			

Sub-scale 3 Supporting and extending language and communication

Item 7 Staff support children's language use

1 2 3 4 5 6 7

	Y	N		Y	N		Y	N		Y	N
1.1	☐	☐	3.1	☐	☐	5.1	☐	☐	7.1	☐	☐
1.2	☐	☐	3.2	☐	☐	5.2	☐	☐	7.2	☐	☐
1.3	☐	☐	3.3	☐	☐	5.3	☐	☐			

Sub-scale 3 Supporting and extending language and communication

Item 8 Sensitive responsiveness

1 2 3 4 5 6 7

	Y	N		Y	N		Y	N		Y	N
1.1	☐	☐	3.1	☐	☐	5.1	☐	☐	7.1	☐	☐
1.2	☐	☐	3.2	☐	☐	5.2	☐	☐	7.2	☐	☐
1.3	☐	☐	3.3	☐	☐	5.3	☐	☐	7.3	☐	☐
1.4	☐	☐									

Sub-scale 4   Supporting learning and critical thinking

Item 9   Supporting curiosity and problem-solving

	1	2	3	4	5	6	7

	Y	N			Y	N			Y	N			Y	N
1.1	☐	☐		3.1	☐	☐		5.1	☐	☐		7.1	☐	☐
1.2	☐	☐		3.2	☐	☐		5.2	☐	☐		7.2	☐	☐
				3.3	☐	☐		5.3	☐	☐		7.3	☐	☐
												7.4	☐	☐

Sub-scale 4   Supporting learning and critical thinking

Item 10   Encouraging sustained shared thinking through storytelling, sharing books, singing, and rhymes

	1	2	3	4	5	6	7

	Y	N			Y	N			Y	N			Y	N
1.1	☐	☐		3.1	☐	☐		5.1	☐	☐		7.1	☐	☐
1.2	☐	☐		3.2	☐	☐		5.2	☐	☐		7.2	☐	☐
				3.3	☐	☐		5.3	☐	☐		7.3	☐	☐
				3.4	☐	☐		5.4	☐	☐				

Sub-scale 4   Supporting learning and critical thinking

Item 11   Encouraging sustained shared thinking in investigation and exploration

	1	2	3	4	5	6	7

	Y	N			Y	N			Y	N			Y	N	N/A
1.1	☐	☐		3.1	☐	☐		5.1	☐	☐		7.1	☐	☐	
1.2	☐	☐		3.2	☐	☐		5.2	☐	☐		7.2	☐	☐	☐
				3.3	☐	☐		5.3	☐	☐		7.3	☐	☐	
								5.4	☐	☐					

Sub-scale 4   Supporting learning and critical thinking

Item 12   Supporting concept development and higher-order thinking   1   2   3   4   5   6   7

	Y	N		Y	N		Y	N		Y	N	N/A
1.1	☐	☐	3.1	☐	☐	5.1	☐	☐	7.1	☐	☐	
			3.2	☐	☐	5.2	☐	☐	7.2	☐	☐	☐
									7.3	☐	☐	
									7.4	☐	☐	

Sub-scale 5   Assessing learning and language

Item 13   Using assessment to support and extend learning and critical thinking   1   2   3   4   5   6   7

	Y	N		Y	N		Y	N		Y	N	N/A
1.1	☐	☐	3.1	☐	☐	5.1	☐	☐	7.1	☐	☐	
1.2	☐	☐	3.2	☐	☐	5.2	☐	☐	7.2	☐	☐	
			3.3	☐	☐	5.3	☐	☐	7.3	☐	☐	☐

Sub-scale 5   Assessing learning and language

Item 14   Assessing language development   1   2   3   4   5   6   7

	Y	N		Y	N		Y	N		Y	N
1.1	☐	☐	3.1	☐	☐	5.1	☐	☐	7.1	☐	☐
			3.2	☐	☐	5.2	☐	☐	7.2	☐	☐
			3.3	☐	☐	5.3	☐	☐			

SSTEW Scale profile

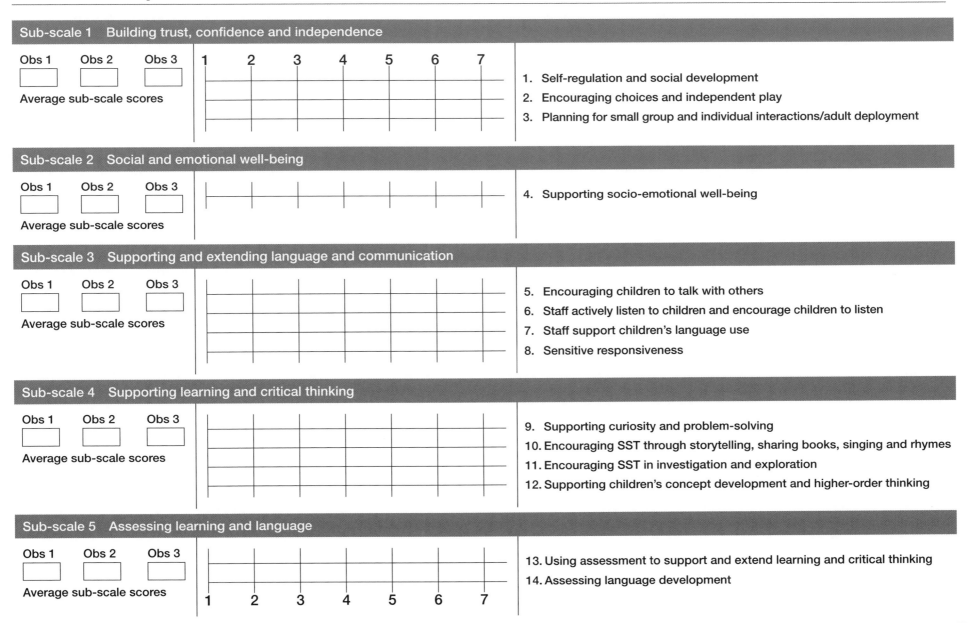

Sub-scale 1   Building trust, confidence and independence

Obs 1   Obs 2   Obs 3

Average sub-scale scores

1   2   3   4   5   6   7

1. Self-regulation and social development
2. Encouraging choices and independent play
3. Planning for small group and individual interactions/adult deployment

Sub-scale 2   Social and emotional well-being

Obs 1   Obs 2   Obs 3

Average sub-scale scores

4. Supporting socio-emotional well-being

Sub-scale 3   Supporting and extending language and communication

Obs 1   Obs 2   Obs 3

Average sub-scale scores

5. Encouraging children to talk with others
6. Staff actively listen to children and encourage children to listen
7. Staff support children's language use
8. Sensitive responsiveness

Sub-scale 4   Supporting learning and critical thinking

Obs 1   Obs 2   Obs 3

Average sub-scale scores

9. Supporting curiosity and problem-solving
10. Encouraging SST through storytelling, sharing books, singing and rhymes
11. Encouraging SST in investigation and exploration
12. Supporting children's concept development and higher-order thinking

Sub-scale 5   Assessing learning and language

Obs 1   Obs 2   Obs 3

Average sub-scale scores

13. Using assessment to support and extend learning and critical thinking
14. Assessing language development

1   2   3   4   5   6   7

Support materials: aspects of child development relevant to the SSTEW Scale

These materials provide some optional information, looking at aspects of children's development, which relate to the practice within the SSTEW Scale. It is not our intention to provide a comprehensive guide to child development or to cover all of the aspects included in the SSTEW Scale. It merely serves as an introduction to some of the underlying developmental notions in the scale, which may be useful to assessors in recognizing practice appropriate to the group of children they are assessing, including those that may have additional learning needs. The age range of children included in the SSTEW Scale is 2–5 years. The information provided below covers a broader age range, from birth to 5 years (and occasionally a little older), as it is recognized that some children will not be achieving at their typically expected level of development. The age ranges covered in the tables below predominantly follow the pattern of: babies (birth to 20 months), toddlers (16–36 months), and young children (30–60 months). These age ranges were first introduced in the UK in relation to the Early Years Professional Status (CWDC, 2010). The age ranges were chosen to deliberately overlap as we recognize that children develop at their own rates and in their own ways. The development statements in the tables and their order are not suggestive of the necessary steps that individual children take, nor are they to be used as checklists of skills in 'ages and stages' that are static. Rather, they are guides to support observations of appropriate practice.

We do not engage with the post-structuralist/modernist debate about child development's use or application within early education here. This is discussed in more detail in Kingston and Siraj (forthcoming), although it is important to point out that we expect practice to be culturally sensitive to the needs of the children in the groups. The SSTEW Scale, as with the family of environment rating scales discussed in the introduction, has its

history based in supporting developmentally appropriate practice in the early years. It is also a response to research that recognizes new ideas and thoughts about effective practice. Our view of child development within the early years is aligned to contemporary developmental theory that is increasingly being recognized by others (e.g. Walsh, 2005; Daniels and Clarkson, 2010; Doherty and Hughes, 2014). The contemporary view of child development argues that effective use of developmental theory requires close attention not only to the individual child but also to the larger socio-cultural context as well as the immediate local context of the setting, including the cultures, beliefs, and expectations within it.

Recent research has pointed to a number of aspects of children's development that are particularly important to support and foster in young children as they have strong continuing effects on children's later socio-emotional and cognitive development. These include developing positive relationships and children's social and emotional well-being in order to support their ability to regulate their emotions, further their executive functioning (such as attentional skills), and promote positive dispositions to learning (Raver et al., 2007; Whitebread, 2012; Siraj and Asani, 2015). The SSTEW Scale considers practice that includes supporting such self-regulation: providing the children with emotional warmth and security, the feelings of self-control and autonomy, and cognitive challenge, together with an articulation of their learning so that they become more aware of their own mental processes of thinking and learning. Interestingly, these appear to be prerequisites to SST, which has been identified as a crucial aspect of excellent practice in settings where children's outcomes improve (Siraj-Blatchford et al., 2002; Siraj-Blatchford, 2009; Sylva et al., 2010).

Below, in sections 1 and 2, we discuss some aspects of social and emotional development, relevant to the age range of 2–5 years, and how this impacts on the SSTEW Scale. In sections 3 and 4 we consider some important cognitive aspects of development: attention development and aspects of language development with links to adult support. These are included to support the recognition of good practice, such as scaffolding children's learning. Finally, there is a short section on play, with links made between play, social development, language development, and attention skills.

1 Social development

We have not considered the whole domain of social development; instead, we have looked at aspects of development that appear to be particularly pertinent to the SSTEW Scale and relevant to the age range of the children included in the scale. Socialization, including sharing, turn-taking, comforting someone who is upset etc. are all relevant here. There is a good deal of evidence that suggests these skills develop with age (e.g. Piaget, 1932; Kohlberg, 1969; Durkin, 1995) and are influenced by how adults nurture children and support them.

Research on pro-social behaviour suggests it is relatively common in young children, especially if it is encouraged and reciprocated. Studies of parenting styles suggest that an authoritative style (not to be confused with an authoritarian style!) supports social and emotional development throughout childhood (Durkin, 1995; Baumrind, 1989; Daglar et al., 2011). Aspects of the authoritative style of parenting can be found within the SSTEW Scale. In particular, the expectation that practitioners would set clear limits and expect and reinforce socially mature behaviour while also being responsive to the children's needs is clearly articulated – that is, practitioners are in control in a warm and nurturing environment.

Within the SSTEW Scale it is also recognized that the ability to follow rules and socialize with others is likely to vary across the age range, with 3- and 4-year-olds being more likely to share and turn-take than children under the age of 3. Thomas (2008) suggests that young children are gradually introduced to the skills of turn-taking and sharing through a progression: first helping the child to 'wait a minute' with adult support, then gradually increasing the waiting time through to taking turns in structured games, and finally in freely chosen activities. The aim being that by the time children reach 5 years of age they should be able to take turns and share confidently. This is reflected in the scale as it considers individual differences and suggests that practice should suit the ability and achievements of the children. Where specific mention is made of the skills of socialization, the indicator is generic enough to apply to all children and a range of abilities; for example, 'Planning shows evidence of learning intentions that are designed to support social interaction, including collaborative activities and play where appropriate' (Sub-scale 2, Item 4, Indicator 5.2).

2 Emotional development

It can be useful to understand aspects of emotional development when supporting children's development and planning for their learning, especially if they are young babies or have additional learning needs. Keenan and Evans (2009) talk about two aspects of emotional development that grow alongside one another: emotional expression and emotional understanding, with emotional expression tending to precede emotional understanding.

Newborn and very young babies' (birth to 20 months) emotional development appears to be limited to emotional expression, which the adults around them interpret. Initially, these emotional expressions are closely linked to reflex responses. So a newborn or young baby may show startle and distress reflexes and express disgust. Then, as they grow and begin to interact with the world and the people around them, they develop the emotional expressions of the social smile, laughter, anger, surprise, sadness, and fear. At some point in their development many, but not all, babies, usually in the second half of their first year, will show 'stranger distress'. 'Stranger distress' is a genuine fear of strangers (Sroufe, 1996) and typically lasts for about two to three months and may even last beyond their first year. 'Stranger distress' can be very concerning for parents and practitioners if they do not understand it as a very natural part of a baby's development, signalling their growing awareness and recognition of main carers, close relatives, and people they meet regularly.

One very important and relatively complex emotional understanding that babies develop is called 'social referencing'. Babies use 'social referencing' to help them understand the world and what is going on around them. They watch other people's emotional responses and expressions (usually people they know well) to support them in interpreting events and situations, especially when they are uncertain or find a situation difficult to grasp or ambiguous. They then mirror the responses and expressions they see. Understanding this could potentially support practitioners in recognizing the importance of making expressions clear and possibly exaggerated to improve meaning and understanding, as well as alerting them to how emotions can be 'catching'.

Toddlers (16–36 months) refine and extend their emotional expressions further by adding shame and pride, typically followed by envy, guilt, and embarrassment, to their repertoires. This is important for practitioners to recognize as these emotional expressions suggest a deeper understanding of self and others and an ability and propensity to compare oneself with others. Such actions would naturally have an impact on children's growing understanding of who they are and on their self-esteem. Typically then, toddlers have mastered the main emotional expressions that they will use

throughout their childhood and beyond. Next they will need to add the emotional understandings that will support their developing friendships and other social relationships as well as their skills in the self-regulation of their emotions.

Most young children (30–60 months) have a full repertoire of emotional expressions and during this period of growth and development they add the understanding of 'emotional display rules'. These are the rules that dictate which emotions are appropriate to express in given circumstances (Saarni et al., 1998). The young child needs to learn which emotions to express when and to accurately 'read' other children's expressions of emotion. This is clearly articulated within the SSTEW Scale.

Interestingly, Keenan and Evans (2009) suggest that young children are incapable of understanding that people can experience two or more emotions consecutively or simultaneously. So if they see people crying and smiling at weddings, presumably expressing aspects of both joy and sadness at the same time, they would probably become very confused. Children of roughly 6 years of age begin to understand sequences of emotions and children of 9 years can understand simultaneous emotions – but only if they are of the same type or valency. For instance, a 9-year-old might be able to explain, 'she hit me and made me angry and upset', and in response to a sequence of events, 'I would be happy to go and surprised if she came too' – but not the actions of the crying and smiling wedding guest. As they grow older – and Keenan and Evans (2009) suggest this is not until about the age of 11 years – children begin to understand that a single event can cause several different feelings simultaneously: 'I hit him because he made me mad, but I felt guilty and worried about the consequences at the same time.' If these are accurate estimations of age and emotional development, it is no wonder that practitioners need to support children's emotional understandings throughout their early childhood.

It is interesting to note that strategies designed to support conflict resolution with young children, such as the six steps to conflict resolution listed here, are consistent with this account of emotional development:

- step one: approach calmly, stopping any hurtful actions
- step two: acknowledge children's feelings
- step three: gather information
- step four: restate the problem
- step five: ask for solutions and choose one
- step six: be prepared to follow up (HighScope, 2014)

First, they are systematic and involve calm adults (recognizing social referencing), they expect the adult to support the recognition and naming of feelings (emotional display rules), they tend to avoid considerations of sequences of emotions (which would be confusing), and they have a strong focus on finding solutions.

Table 1: Development of emotional expression and understanding, showing typical order of development and rough age ranges

(Note: this guide is designed to support observation of practice and planning.)

Age	Emotional expressions	Emotional understanding
Newborn/very young baby	• Startle, disgust, distress	
Baby (0–20 months)	• Social smile • Laughter, anger, interest, surprise, sadness • Fear • Stranger distress	• Social referencing
Toddler (16–36 months)	• Shame, pride • Envy, guilt, embarrassment	
Young children (30–60 months)		• Emotional display rules
6–8 years		• Awareness that two emotions can occur in sequence
9 years-plus		• Awareness that emotions of the same valency can occur simultaneously
11 years		• Awareness that one event can elicit a range of feelings

Adapted from Keenan and Evans, 2009

3 Cognitive development

3a Cognitive development: attention

Attention, as discussed in the introductory paragraphs of this appendix, is seen as an important aspect of self-regulation. It also follows a developmental trajectory and will affect children's ability to respond to peers and adults, to concentrate on activities and follow rules.

The following table is based on the work of Cooper et al. (1978), who originally researched the development of attention, together with information adapted from other sources such as Development Matters in the Early Years Foundation Stage (EYFS) (Early Education, 2012). The development of attention involves two important aspects: an increase in the 'fine tuning' of attention as well as its flexibility. The SSTEW Scale is sensitive to the development of attention, recognizing that attention skills may vary from single channelled attention to alternating attention to multichannelled attention. It is also sensitive to individual differences and recognizes that some children need to be supported to maintain attention and to switch attention between different foci.

Table 2: Development of attention, showing typical order and rough ages

(Note: this guide is designed to support observation of practice and planning.)

Attention
Babies (0–20 months)
• Initially, child's **attention flits** from one object, person, or event to another and the baby is easily distracted.
• Gradually, the child begins to focus on one aspect of the environment (**single channelled attention**), but cannot tolerate any interruptions.
Toddlers (16–36 months)
• Initially, toddlers show **single channelled attention**. They can concentrate on an activity of their own choosing but cannot tolerate any verbal or non-verbal interruptions. At this stage, they are unlikely to hear an adult asking them to tidy up now.
• Gradually, with an adult's help, they can move between activities, e.g. while playing a game if the adult touches them lightly on the arm they will respond and look at the adult and listen. Once the message has been heard, they can return to their game if the adult redirects them to it. They can **alternate attention with support**.
Young children (30–60 months)
• Initially, young children of this age still show single channelled attention but are able to **alternate attention spontaneously** without an adult supporting focus.
• Gradually, attention becomes **two channelled**, so that young children can be playing and also hear and attend to instructions. Their attention span might be **short** but group instruction is possible.
• The final stage of attention (which may not be achieved by the age of 5 years) is when attention becomes **multichannelled, well established, and maintained**. Auditory, visual, and manipulatory channels of attention are integrated. Gradually, young children are able to shut out unwanted irrelevant information and concentrate on essential aspects of the environment spontaneously.

Adapted from Cooper et al., 1978

3b Cognitive development: language development

Children's language development within the age range covered by the SSTEW Scale will vary a great deal, and although the development of language described here is linked to age ranges, this is not the important element. The information provided is designed to support the assessment of spoken or expressive language in order to support practice and plan for the adult's role in supporting the children's next steps in learning. The table includes brief descriptions of the children's expressive language, together with a brief summary of the adult's role in relation to the children's achievements.

The range of expressive language skills found within early childhood settings is likely to vary: some children are pre-verbal, others may use single words, yet others may use two- or three-word combinations, some will use simple sentences, and finally, some may use longer and more complex sentences and be able to hold long conversations. The scale recognizes this diversity and considers practice that supports and scaffolds children's learning according to their individual needs.

Table 3: A brief outline of typical language development, showing typical order and rough age ranges as well as describing some of the practice that supports development

1. Discoverer (0–8 months)	Initially, communication is by reflex. The baby then becomes really interested in others, wanting attention, showing feelings, intentions, and imitating others. *I cry, smile, make sounds, follow your gaze.*	The adults must interpret meaning for babies. They should talk to babies and engage in child-directed speech. As the babies develop, the adults imitate their sounds and add new sounds. The babies respond and simple sequences of repeating sounds and interactions begin. The adults add new actions to games, e.g. peek-a-boo, with hands, hats etc. Sing songs and rhymes. Adults create new simple routines and use daily routines: feeding, changing, dressing, as opportunities to communicate.
2. Communicator (8–13 months)	Babies send purposeful messages directly to others. They use a combination of eye gaze, facial expression, sounds, and gestures. The baby becomes very sociable. *I make sounds, I look, make gestures, and 'talk'.*	The adults help the babies to learn a word or two. They use gestures, particularly pointing, to support understanding. They repeat language related to routines: more, out, in, up, bye-bye, gone. They interpret a range of purposes for communication: you want, like, tired, hungry. They begin to add pretend toys to play, e.g. cup for self-play. They demonstrate simple pretend play with large toys. They share photo picture books, engage with turn-taking games with balls or shakers, play hiding games, and give push-and-go toys.

3. First words user (12–18 months)	Babies crack the 'language code' and begin to use single words. *I am learning more and more single words.*	The adults provide useful labels for objects and actions. They provide key word commentaries on babies' play. They give verbal choices (also known as forced alternatives) e.g. 'shoes or socks?', 'milk or juice?', 'car or book?' – i.e. give choices while offering two items. NB: They do not withhold an item. If the child does not respond, they make their best guess. They start a sentence and let the child finish it: 'it's going in the … [box]'. They continue with play, books, games etc. as before.
4. Combiner (18–24 months)	Toddlers show a big increase in vocabulary and begin to combine words. They also start to take more turns in interactions. *I am making simple 'sentences' using two words, and a combination of intonation, gesture, and context.*	The adults engage in more and longer spoken interactions. They provide key phrase commentaries on children's play. They support and add to play. They give verbal choices (also known as forced alternatives), e.g. 'shoes on or socks on?', 'more milk or more juice?', 'teddy jump or teddy sit?'. They start a sentence and let them finish: 'rabbits going … [in the box]'. They repeat what children say, adding an extra word or two.
5. Early sentence user (2–3 years)	Toddlers progress from two-word to five-word sentences and can now hold short conversations. *I am making simple sentences and can bring ideas together to hold a conversation.*	The adults listen to and extend stories and play. The adults support understanding of language related to concepts, e.g. in, on, under, big, little, long, empty, wet, hard, first, same. The adults also support collaborative and pretend play.
6. Later sentence user (3–5 years)	Young children use long and complex sentences and can hold long conversations. *I can share my thoughts and experiences, use my imagination in play, ask questions, and follow simple instructions.*	The adults support language and thought in longer conversations. The adults support problem-solving, reflecting, and evaluating activities. They ask questions that support thinking. The adults support learning through different types of play, making choices, setting challenges, socio-dramatic collaborative play etc. The adults read stories and narratives, model thinking skills and language, extend play by taking on roles, providing props etc.

Adapted from Hanen's third A, Adding to the children's language (Weitzman and Greenberg, 2002)

4 Play

4a Play: social participation in play

Play is considered to be an important vehicle for learning, fundamental to children's all-round development and critical for practitioners to understand if they are to sensitively support and extend thinking and learning and engage in SST. Play, and the adult's role in relation to it, are key aspects of the SSTEW Scale. There are a large number of informative and accomplished authors and editors who publish extensively on play within early childhood education and care (e.g. Moyles, 2010; Broadhead et al., 2010). Here we do not intend to discuss play in detail; we limit our discussions to children's social participation followed by early play development and finally we consider some of the aspects of development that dramatic and socio-dramatic play may support and how this could impact on practice.

Play has been recognized as important within early childhood for a great many years. We begin with a consideration of how children's play and social participation interlink, drawing upon Parten's (1932) categories of play behaviour. Parten, a pioneer in play, studied 2–5-year-olds as they played. She found that the frequency of social activity in play increased with age, so that older children were more likely to be seen engaging in collaborative play. These classifications are still relevant today as more contemporary work suggests (e.g. Siraj and Asani, 2015). Subsequent to Parten's work, and supporting her initial thoughts on play, the most frequent type of play found in settings for 3- and 4-year-olds was discovered to be parallel play, which was believed to be a precursor to collaborative play (Bakeman and Brownlee, 1982). However, within the SSTEW Scale, diversity and individual children's needs are recognized and so opportunities and support for all types of social participation play are encouraged.

Table 4: The development of social participation play linked to age ranges

(Note: these may be seen during observations, and expectations and practice within play may differ with different age ranges.)

Parten, 1932 (six categories of social participation play for children aged 2–5 years)
Unoccupied behaviour: The children are not playing but may pay fleeting attention to activities progressing around them; that is, they are waiting and apparently doing very little. (**toddlers 16–36 months and young children 30–60 months**)
Solitary play: The children are playing alone, their play is individual and they pay little to no attention to other children around them and their activities. (**toddlers 16–36 months**)
Onlooker behaviour: The children watch other children play. They may speak to others but not join in, e.g. watches another. (**toddlers 16–36 months and young children 30–60 months**)
Parallel play: The children play alongside others, engaging in similar activities. They may imitate others but no true interaction and no joint agreed goal can be seen. (**toddlers 16–36 months and young children 30–60 months**)
Associative play: The children share resources with other children, but there are no real roles or scenarios developed. (**young children 30–60 months**)
Co-operative play: The children play as part of a group. Play includes games with rules, role play, model making together. (**young children 30–60 months or older**)

Adapted from Parten, 1932

The SSTEW Scale recognizes that children may wish to play alone, side by side, or together in small or larger groups and this may be dependent on the context as much as the child's individual development, previous experiences, and achievements, which is why practice and the environment should allow for all levels of social participation in play. The SSTEW Scale promotes this, but also notes the progression in social participation play and how important it is for practitioners to understand this in order to support effective practice, which includes scaffolding and supporting play as it develops.

4b Play: early play development

As well as providing opportunities for play and valuing play, the SSTEW Scale considers whether practitioners take an active and sensitive role in children's play, encouraging practice that supports adults being invited to play. It includes consideration of practice that allows children to take the lead and respects the level of play and rules established by the children. In addition, it considers the importance of supporting children and enhancing and deepening their play, which necessitates an understanding of how play develops as well as an ability to assess and plan for play.

Table 5: Shows the progression of play according to McConkey (no date) from birth to 3 years

(Note: this table could potentially support practitioners' engagement in and the assessment of the play of younger children as well as with older children in need of additional support in engaging in play.)

Early explorations and play in babies, toddlers, and younger children
Babies (0–20 months)
• **Exploratory play:** Initially, babies explore objects, their bodies, and the surroundings by mouthing, examining, feeling, rubbing, shaking, hitting objects on the wall, floor etc., dropping (and looking), throwing, swiping, manipulating parts of objects.
• **Relational play:** Later, babies engage in relational play, exploring objects' physical properties and/or their use. Exploring physical properties includes: banging two objects together (while holding both objects), placing one object into or on top of another, taking rings off or placing rings onto a stack, building a tower of two cubes. Exploring objects by use includes: putting a spoon into a cup, a pillow onto a bed, a sheet on a bed, cloth on a table, chair next to a table, brushing or combing hair.
Babies (0–20 months) and toddlers (16–36 months)
• **Self-pretend play:** (This typically develops after exploratory and relational play.) Examples: feeds self with cup, spoon, makes feeding sounds, brushes hair, washes self, sleeps on doll's bed or pillow, sits on doll's chair, dresses self with dolls clothes etc. We know that it is play because it occurs in situations and at times outside of the normal routine, e.g. pretends to eat when it is not dinner time.
• **Doll pretending:** (This marks the first decentred play, i.e. pretend not focused on the self. Play can be relational or not.) Examples of relational play: feeds doll with cup/spoon, combs/brushes doll's hair, washes doll, lies doll on bed/pillow, sits doll on chair, dresses/undresses doll. Examples of doll alone: kisses doll, walks doll, makes doll jump.
Toddlers (16–36 months) and young children (30–60 months)
• **Sequence pretending:** (This can be either a sequence of the same action or along a theme.) Examples of same action: feeds doll/self/adult, combs hair of doll/self/adult, sleeps doll/self/adult, phones doll/self/adult. Examples of a theme: feeding sequence, sleeping sequence, bathing sequence, ironing sequence etc.

McConkey (no date)

It is interesting to note how language development links and appears to be related to play, as it supports the notion of using play to support language development (see Example and supplementary notes for Sub-scale 5: Assessing learning and language, Item 14: Assessing language development, Indicator 7.1. 'Staff recognize that supporting children's play is effective in supporting language development. They observe the effect of scaffolding children's learning and supporting them to engage in more interaction with others and more complex imaginative play').

In relation to the table above, it is interesting to note that children who typically engage in exploratory play are at the pre-symbolic language stage and use vocalizations and gestures to indicate their needs. Those who engage in relational play are at the symbolic stage, where they have cracked the language code and are beginning to use words meaningfully. Those who engage in self-pretend play are still very centred on themselves (that is, play typically involves them taking the central role rather than dolls or other toys being the main subject, the hero etc.), but are extending the number of words they can use. As they reach the decentred play of doll pretending/other pretending, they begin to combine words into two-word sentences and as they engage in sequence pretending they also start to talk in multiword sentences. There seems to be a link in the complexity of thought with both play and language use that could be usefully applied to practice.

4c Play: young children's dramatic and socio-dramatic play development

As children's play matures, more complex dramatic (alone) and socio-dramatic (with one or more play partners) play is often seen when children are given the opportunity to play and use their imaginations. This is not to say that younger children do not engage in this type of play – many will naturally choose to do so and others can be successfully supported in doing so. The SSTEW Scale supports the practice of playing with children at and slightly beyond their individual play level, thus scaffolding their learning.

Wood and Attfield (2005) suggested that children demonstrate a number of skills, dispositions, and competences during dramatic and socio-dramatic play. They developed a framework of these skills, dispositions, and competences – not to be used as a hierarchy or checklist, but as a way of sensitizing practitioners to the complexities of play, including the social, emotional, and cognitive demands within episodes of play and also as a useful guide when developing individual play plans. Wood and Attfield's (2005) framework was used to support the development of the framework here (see Table 6). As with the original, it is not designed to be used as a checklist but as a useful guide to support the assessment of and planning for this type of play. In relation to the SSTEW Scale, it is hoped that the framework may act as a guide to the aspects of development typically found in dramatic and socio-dramatic play and the areas of learning that practitioners may support here.

Table 6 illustrates how dramatic and socio-dramatic play may support children's learning across the developmental domains of cognitive, social-emotional, and motor development. It could also serve as an aide-mémoire for practitioners who wish to support and extend children's play and learning here. Throughout the SSTEW Scale, practice is considered that promotes both self-regulation and metacognitive abilities in children (2–5 years). In particular, the sensitive use and role of interaction during play and the medium of language are emphasized as important aspects of SST, and are seen as useful in supporting children's thinking and learning.

Note: assessment in the early years

The final sub-scale in the SSTEW Scale considers practice associated with assessment in early childhood education and care provision (see Glazzard et al., 2010; Nutbrown and Carter, 2010; Nutbrown, 2011). The indicators link to both assessment of learning and assessment for learning, with an emphasis on the latter (Black et al., 2003). How the indicators are linked to practice and the underlying research and evidence, together with further illustrations and examples, are discussed in detail in Kingston and Siraj (forthcoming).

Table 6: Framework for dramatic and socio-dramatic play of a child

Cognitive aspects: memory, attention, imagination, creativity, and information processing	Cognitive aspects: communication and language	Social and emotional aspects	Motor development etc.
• Uses memory to develop play • Observes closely and carefully • Transforms objects, materials, environment, and actions • Distances (steps in and out of play) • Rehearses (roles, actions) and directs or manages own play • Maintains and develops a role/play • Uses imagination and creativity to combine and recombine ideas • Creates, identifies, and solves problems • Reveals motives, needs, and interests • Uses metacognitive strategies – predicts, monitors, checks, reflects, evaluates • Takes risks, refines ideas, edits work/products • Distinguishes fantasy and reality • Combines fantasy and reality	• Defines a theme – characters, plot, and sequence (story) • Communicates representational thinking (using language, signs, symbols, and gestures) • Communicates pretence/metacommunication (defines roles and actions, conveys meaning and intentions) • Communicates with peers and adults in small and large groups • Uses descriptive language to convey experience, feelings and ideas, to organize, persuade and report accurately • Uses specific terms to describe and analyse experience (e.g. mathematical, scientific, technological)	• Negotiates a play frame (establishes environment and rules) • Gives ideas and listens to others • Negotiates and co-operates towards agreed ends • Rehearses (roles, actions) and directs or manages others in play • Allows direction and management by others • Shows empathy towards others • Uses conflict-resolution strategies • Listens, co-operates, revises, and extends ideas • Seeks help from adults/peers • Regulates own feelings and emotions • Responds emotionally to experiences and expresses emotions verbally and through different media • Establishes friendships – same and opposite sex	• Uses gross motor skills (dependent on play) • Uses fine motor skills in investigating, controlling, and manipulating materials • Represents ideas through different media (drawing, painting modelling, writing, construction, and layouts etc.) • Combines materials and resources • Uses a variety of tools to assist investigation • Enjoys sensory experiences

Developed from Wood and Attfield, 2005.

Joint observation/inter-rater reliability for the SSTEW Scale

Centre observed _____ Date _____

Group of children/room _____ Teachers/practitioners _____

Observers _____

Names of observers					Agreed final score
Building trust, confidence and independence					
1. Self-regulation and social development					
2. Encouraging choices and independent play					
3. Planning for small group and individual interactions/adult deployment					
Social and emotional well-being					
4. Supporting socio-emotional well-being					
Supporting and extending language and communication					
5. Encouraging children to talk with others					
6. Staff actively listen to children and encourage children to listen					
7. Staff support children's language use					
8. Sensitive responsiveness					
Supporting learning and critical thinking					
9. Supporting curiosity and problem-solving					
10. Encouraging sustained shared thinking through storytelling, sharing books, singing, and rhymes					
11. Encouraging sustained shared thinking in investigation and exploration					
12. Supporting concept development and higher-order thinking					
Assessing learning and language					
13. Using assessment to support and extend learning and critical thinking					
14. Assessing language development					

References

Bakeman, R. and Brownlee, J. (1982) 'The strategic use of parallel play: A sequential analysis'. *Child Development*, 51, 873–8.

Baumrind, D. (1989) 'Rearing competent children'. In W. Damon (ed.), *Child Development Today and Tomorrow*. San Francisco: Jossey-Bass.

Black, P., Harrison, C., Lee, C., Marshall, B., and Wiliam, D. (2003) *Assessment for Learning, Putting It into Practice*. Maidenhead: Open University Press.

Broadhead, P., Howard, J., and Wood, E. (eds) (2010) *Play and Learning in the Early Years*. London: Sage.

Burchinal, M., Peisner-Feinberg, E., Pianta, R., and Howes, C. (2002) 'Development of academic skills from preschool through second grade: Family and classroom predictors of developmental trajectories'. *Journal of School Psychology*, 40 (5), 415–36.

Burchinal, M., Nelson, L., Carlson, M., and Brooks-Gunn, J. (2008) 'Neighborhood characteristics, and child care type and quality'. *Early Education & Development*, 19 (5), 702–25.

Cooper, J., Moodley, M., and Reynell, J. (1978) *Helping Language Development: A developmental programme for children with early learning handicaps*. London: Edward Arnold.

CWDC (Children's Workforce Development Council) (2010) 'On the Right Track: Guidance to the standards for the award of early years professional status'. Online. *http://webarchive.nationalarchives. gov.uk/20110908152055/http://www.cwdcouncil.org.uk/ assets/0000/9008/Guidance_To_Standards.pdf* (accessed September 2014).

Daglar, M., Melhuish, E., and Barnes, J. (2011) 'Parenting and preschool child behaviour amongst Turkish immigrant, migrant and non-migrant families'. *European Journal of Developmental Psychology*, 8, 261–79.

Daniels, D.H. and Clarkson, P.K. (2010) *A Developmental Approach to Educating Young Children*. London: Sage.

DEEWR (Department of Education, Employment and Workplace Relations) and CAG (Council of Australian Governments) (2009) 'Belonging, Being and Becoming: The early years learning framework for Australia'. Online. http://docs.education.gov.au/system/files/doc/ other/belonging_being_and_becoming_the_early_years_learning_ framework_for_australia.pdf (accessed September 2009).

Doherty, J. and Hughes, M. (2014) *Child Development Theory and Practice 0–11*, 2nd ed. Harlow: Pearson Education.

Durkin, K. (1995) *Developmental Social Psychology: From infancy to old age*. Oxford: Blackwell.

Early Education (2012) 'Development Matters in the Early Years Foundation Stage'. Online. www.foundationyears.org.uk/ files/2012/03/Development-Matters-FINAL-PRINT-AMENDED. pdf (accessed September 2014).

Glazzard, J., Chadwick, D., Webster, A., and Percival. J. (2010) *Assessment for Learning in the Early Years Foundation Stage*. London: Sage.

Harms, T., Clifford, R.M., and Cryer, D. (2005) *Early Childhood Environment Rating Scale–Revised Edition* (ECERS-R). New York: Teachers College Press.

Harms, T., Clifford, R.M., and Cryer, D. (2003) *Infant/Toddler Environment Rating Scale* (ITERS-R). New York: Teachers College Press.

HighScope (2014) 'Social Development'. Online. www.highscope.org/Content.asp?ContentId=294 (accessed 12 September 2014).

Howes, C., Burchinal, M., Pianta, R., Bryant, D., Early, D., Clifford, R., and Barbarin, O. (2008) 'Ready to learn? Children's pre-academic achievement in pre-Kindergarten programs'. *Early Childhood Research Quarterly*, 23, 27–50.

Keenan, T. and Evans, S. (2009) *An Introduction to Child Development*, 2nd ed. London: Sage.

Kingston, D. and Siraj, I. (forthcoming) *Powerful Pedagogies: Enhancing quality interactions and well-being through early childhood education*. London: IOE Press.

Kohlberg, L. (1969) 'Stage and sequence: The cognitive developmantal approach to socialisation'. In D.A. Goslin (ed.), *Handbook of Socialisation Theory and Research*. Chicago: Rand McNally.

Mashburn, A.J., Pianta, R.C., Hamre, B.K., Downer, J.T., Barbarin, O.A., Bryant, D., Burchinal, M., Early, D., and Howes, C. (2008) 'Measures of classroom quality in prekindergarten and children's development of academic, language, and social skills'. *Child Development*, 79 (3), 732–49.

McConkey (no date) Closest reference: Jeffree, D.M., McConkey, R., and Hewson, S. (1977) *Let Me Play*. London: Souvenir Press.

Melhuish, E.C. (2004) *Child Benefits: The importance of investing in quality childcare*. London: Daycare Trust.

Moyles, J. (ed.) (2010) *The Excellence of Play*. Maidenhead: Open University Press.

Nutbrown, C. (2011) 'Chapter 9: Assessment for learning'. In C. Nutbrown, *Threads of Thinking*, 4th ed. London: Sage.

Nutbrown, C. and Carter, C. (2010) 'Watching and listening: The tools of assessment'. In G. Pugh and B. Duffy (eds), *Contemporary Issues in the Early Years*, 5th ed. London: Paul Chapman Publishing.

Parten, M. (1932) 'Social participation among pre-school children'. *Journal of Abnormal and Social Psychology*, 27, 243–69.

Phillipsen, L.C., Burchinal, M.R., Howes, C., and Cryer, D. (1997) 'The prediction of process quality from structural features of child care'. *Early Childhood Research Quarterly*, 12, 281–303.

Piaget, J. (1932) *The Moral Judgement of the Child*. Harmondsworth: Penguin.

Raver, C., Garner, P., and Smith-Donald, R. (2007) 'The roles of emotional regulation and emotional knowledge for children's academic readiness: Are there causal links?' In R. Pianta, M. Cox, and K. Snow (eds), *School Readiness and the Transition to Kindergarten in the Era of Accountability*. Baltimore: Paul H. Brookes.

Saarni, C., Mumme, D.L., and Campos, J.J. (1998) 'Emotional development: Action, communication and understanding'. In W. Damon (gen. ed.) and N. Eisenberg (vol. ed.), *Handbook of Child Psychology: Vol. 3. Social, emotional, and personality development*. New York: Wiley.

Siraj, I. and Asani, R. (2015) 'The role of sustained shared thinking, play and metacognition in young children's learning'. In S. Robson and S. Quinn (eds), *The Routledge International Handbook of Young Children's Thinking and Understanding*. London: Routledge.

Siraj-Blatchford, I. (2009) 'Conceptualising progression in the pedagogy of play and sustained shared thinking in early childhood education: A Vygotskian perspective'. *Educational and Child Psychology*, 26 (2), 77–89.

Siraj-Blatchford, I., Sylva, K., Muttock, S., Gilden, R., and Bell, D. (2002) *Researching Effective Pedagogy in the Early Years (REPEY): DfES Research Report 356*. London: DfES.

Sroufe, L.A. (1996) *Emotional Development. The Organisation of Emotional Life in the Early Years*. New York: Wiley.

Study of Early Education and Development (SEED). Online. www.seed. natcen.ac.uk/ (accessed September 2014).

Sylva, K., Melhuish, E., Sammons, P., Siraj-Blatchford, I., and Taggart, B. (2004) *Effective Pre-school Provision*. London: DfES.

Sylva, K., Siraj-Blatchford, I., and Taggart, B. (2010) *Assessing Quality in the Early Years: Early Childhood Environment Rating Scale–Extension (ECERS-E): Four curricular sub-scales*, rev. 4th ed. New York: Teachers' College Press.

Thomas, S. (2008) *Nurturing Babies and Children Under Four*. London: Heinemann.

Walsh, D. (2005) 'Developmental theory and early childhood education: Necessary but not sufficient'. In N. Yelland (ed.), *Critical Issues in Early Childhood Education*. Maidenhead: Open University Press.

Weitzman, E. and Greenberg, J. (2002) *Learning Language and Loving It*. Toronto: Hanen Centre.

Whitebread, D. (2012) *Developmental Psychology and Early Childhood Education*. London: Sage.

Wood, E. and Attfield, J. (2005) *Play, Learning and the Early Childhood Curriculum*, 2nd ed. London: Sage.